100

THINGS TO DO IN
ANN ARBOR
BEFORE YOU
DIE

MW00573255

100
THINGS TO DO IN
ANN ARBOR
BEFORE YOU
DIE

• •

PATRICIA MAJHER

Copyright © 2020 by Reedy Press, LLC
Reedy Press
PO Box 5131
St. Louis, MO 63139, USA
www.reedypress.com

No part of this publication may be reproduced or transmitted in any form or by any means, electronic or mechanical, including photocopy, recording, or any information storage and retrieval system, without permission in writing from the publisher.

Permissions may be sought directly from Reedy Press at the above mailing address or via our website at www.reedypress.com.

Library of Congress Control Number: 2020937357

ISBN: 9781681062655

Design by Jill Halpin

Shutterstock photos, pages ii, vi, 54, and 78.

Printed in the United States of America
20 21 22 23 24   5 4 3 2 1

We (the publisher and the author) have done our best to provide the most accurate information available when this book was completed. However, we make no warranty, guaranty or promise about the accuracy, completeness or currency of the information provided, and we expressly disclaim all warranties, express or implied. Please note that attractions, company names, addresses, websites, and phone numbers are subject to change or closure, and this is outside of our control. We are not responsible for any loss, damage, injury, or inconvenience that may occur due to the use of this book. When exploring new destinations, please do your homework before you go. You are responsible for your own safety and health when using this book.

• •

DEDICATION

To my sister, Connie Devereaux, whose love of Ann Arbor's
fairy doors was an inspiration for this book.

• •

CONTENTS

Music and Entertainment

Sports and Recreation

Culture and History

• •

• •

• •

PREFACE

When I began to develop this book, I reached out to friends who are longtime Ann Arbor residents and asked, "What's most important for me to include in these pages?" Answers came back in a flood, covering a wide variety of subjects. But there were three things that almost everyone mentioned: the art fairs, the University of Michigan, and the Kerrytown area including Zingerman's Delicatessen.

As a result, these things received more than adequate attention in *100 Things to Do in Ann Arbor Before You Die*. But I didn't stop there. I included out-of-the-way restaurants, under-the-radar shops, and almost-undiscovered cultural, entertainment, and recreational activities. (Case in point: I couldn't believe how many people didn't know we have competitive roller derby teams in our midst!) In the end, I believe, I struck a balance between the familiar and the fresh—a phrase that perfectly describes Ann Arbor to me.

I hope you enjoy the fruits of my labor and that you plan a trip to visit Ann Arbor very soon!

ACKNOWLEDGMENTS

I'm indebted to our local print media—the *Ann Arbor News*, the *Ann Arbor Observer*, *Current* magazine, and the *Michigan Daily*—as well as Destination Ann Arbor, publishers of the *Ann Arbor Area Visitors Guide*, for providing me with a place to start my research. Writer Grace Shackman was a wonderful additional resource for all things historical.

I also appreciate the input of two dear friends, natives of the city, who offered the benefit of their lifelong association with it: Cathy Hunter and Ruth Anne Southgate. Simone Strong and Elizabeth Thompson have dedicated many years of selfless service to the Ann Arbor area and provided me with a wealth of ideas that guided my writing.

Last but not least, Anna Darnell and Paul Feeny helped bring a fresh (and young!) perspective to this travel guide.

FOOD AND DRINK

SAMPLE
CENTRAL EUROPE
AT AMADEUS

As you step through the door and part the red-velvet drapes, you immediately feel it: you've left Ann Arbor for the charming atmosphere of a European street café. Amadeus's décor contributes to this impression, with musical instruments and portraits of famous composers on the wall. But it's the dining options that make it real. Third-generation restaurateur Pavel Strozynski has crafted a menu of classic dishes from Poland, Hungary, and Austria including paprikash, goulash, pierogi, potato pancakes, and dill-pickle soup. Complementing these is an array of European wines, liqueurs, and beers. But save room for dessert; the house-made tortes and gateaux are "to dine for." An Amadeus extra: live classical music on Friday and Saturday evenings.

122 E. Washington St.
(734) 665-8767
amadeusrestaurant.com

GET SCHOOLED
IN FINE FOOD AT GARRETT'S

Longing to sample gourmet foods without the gourmet prices? Then make your way to Garrett's, the teaching restaurant associated with Washtenaw Community College's culinary arts program. Under the watchful eyes of expert faculty, students handle every aspect of operating this establishment, from planning the menus to preparing the food to serving it with a smile tableside. Menus change weekly, with imaginative appetizers, soups, salads, sandwiches, and entrees. (A vegetarian example of the latter: sweet potato gnocchi cooked in brown butter and served with wilted spinach, toasted walnuts, apples, and a cider vinegar gastrique. Yum.) Next door at The Sweet Spot, you can purchase a box of scratch-made delights prepared in the college's baking and pastry classes.

132 Student Center Building
4800 E. Huron River Dr.
(734) 973-3592
culinary.wccnet.edu/garrets

TIP
Garrett's is open during fall and winter semesters for lunch and dinner on varying days. Check the website for specifics.

EXPERIENCE ETHIOPIA
AT THE BLUE NILE

Want to try something truly new? The Blue Nile restaurant offers the city's most unique dining experience. To honor Ethiopia's tradition of *gursha*, eating from the same plate and sharing the same bread, the restaurant's chef prepares a special, savory feast combining seven vegetable side dishes with chicken and beef. (Lamb can be added for an extra charge.) The food arrives on a single large platter and is set on a circular table for all to reach. The preferred way to enjoy this feast is to tear off a piece of injera, a spongy flatbread, and use it to scoop the food into your mouth. But you can ask for utensils if you prefer. All of the feast's items are also available as entrées, and Ethiopian wine is also on the menu.

211 E. Washington St.
(734) 998-4746
bluenilemi.com

FILL UP
AT AN ALL-VEGAN EATERY

Across the street from Kerrytown is a restaurant named for its building's original purpose. Detroit Street Filling Station doesn't sell gas anymore, but it does fill its patrons with made-from-scratch, all-vegan dishes that are both delicious and nutritious. A prime example is *japchae*, a sweet-potato noodle stir-fry with spinach, shiitake mushrooms, onion, red bell pepper, carrot, scallions, sesame, and a splash of lime juice. The restaurant's beverage menu really shines, too. Among its original craft cocktails is one dedicated to Ann Arbor—the A2 Mule—made with vodka, ginger, lime, and lemon-lime soda. Imagine how refreshing that would be with Sunday brunch on a sunlit patio with your faithful Fido by your side! The patio is enclosed for comfort in the winter, and live music completes the picture year-round.

300 Detroit St.
(734) 224-2161
detroitstreetfillingstation.com

ENJOY FRENCH FOOD
AT THE SURPRISING SPENCER

To place an order at Spencer, you go to the counter, tell the staff what you want, pick up a flag stand, and seat yourself along one of two long communal tables. When your meal is ready, a runner brings it out. Sound like the latest fast-casual eatery? It's not. It's fine dining 2.0, with a menu of French-inspired small plates that recently made a reviewer from the *New York Times* positively gush. (She must have sampled the pork pelmeni with dill crème fraîche and pickled cherries.) Spencer's owners are equally committed to fine wines, with an expertly curated collection that is rotated nightly. For connoisseurs, there's a wine club to enjoy. For adventuresome amateurs, Thursday-night tastings highlight new arrivals, producer features, unique varietals, and staff favorites.

113 E. Liberty St.
(734) 369-3979
spencerannarbor.com

TIP

Spencer has limited hours. The restaurant opens its doors for dinner five nights a week and brunch on the weekends, and is closed on Tuesdays and Wednesdays.

COME TOGETHER
AT A COOL COCKTAIL LOUNGE

You're walking west up Huron Street and come upon an unmarked door. If you're curious enough to give the handle a pull and walk down the stairs, you'll find yourself in one of Ann Arbor's premier cocktail bars: The Last Word. TLW's beverage menu—literally a book—devotes three of its six chapters to mixed drinks. That's where you'll find the bar's namesake beverage made with gin, green Chartreuse, maraschino liqueur, and fresh lime.

301 W. Huron St., (734) 623-1443
thelastwordbar.com

A couple of blocks away, Nightcap, which employs innovative technologies (centrifuges!) and new-school bartending techniques, also breathes new life into a Tom Collins by combining rosemary-infused gin with grapefruit, honey, and soda. On Washington Street, Mash stays true to its name by specializing in whiskey-based cocktails. Ever had a mint julep enhanced with allspice and agave nectar?

Nightcap
220 S. Main St., (734) 369-6070
nightcapbara2.com

Mash
211 E. Washington St., (734) 222-4095
mashbar.net

Babs' Underground elevates its cocktails with imaginative additions of fruit flavoring. Case in point: the Punch Drunk with rum, raspberries, lime, simple syrup, bitters, and champagne. The Alley Bar, which calls itself a "relaxed cocktail bar or an upscale dive," takes the opposite tack with its signature beverage, the Pickleback: a shot of Irish whiskey chased with (did you guess it?) pickle brine!

Babs' Underground
213 S. Ashley St., (734) 997-0800
babsannarbor.com

Alley Bar
112 W. Liberty St., (734) 662-8757
alleybarannarbor.com

TIP

It's not a cocktail lounge per se. But the tasting room of the Ann Arbor Distilling Company serves cocktails to showcase its handcrafted gin, vodka, whiskey, fruit and coffee liqueurs, schnapps, absinthe, and cherry eau de vie.

220 Felch St.
(734) 882-2169
annarbordistilling.com

SAVOR THE FLAVORS
OF CUBAN-STYLE FRITA BATIDOS

Eve Aronoff, a *Top Chef* contestant and cookbook author, drew inspiration for her fun restaurant Frita Batidos from childhood visits to Miami. She calls the menu "Cuban-inspired street food." You'll call it delicious.

Start by picking your favorite frita (traditionally a chorizo burger, but you can also choose chicken, black bean, beef, or fish) from the menu. Next add a side like plantains, a tropical slaw, or Eve's "best snack ever": coconut-ginger rice layered with black beans, melted Muenster cheese, and a cilantro-lime salsa. Then round out your meal with a batido, a tropical milkshake made with fruit, crushed ice, and vanilla ice cream. (Some say batidos taste best with a splash of rum, and the waitstaff can make that happen.) Menu-matching mixed drinks, beers, and juices are also available.

117 W. Washington St.
(734) 761-2882
fritabatidos.com

NOSH YOUR WAY
THROUGH A WALKING TOUR

Planning a trip to A2, but have only a short time to explore its famous foodie culture? Your best bet is to take a By the Sidewalk Food Tour. On weekends from March through December, founder Aniruddh Gala or one of his city-savvy guides leads walking tours that meander through downtown, the State and Liberty shopping district, and other areas of the city.

Along the way, you'll have a chance to sample steamed bao buns, trendy tacos, and French macarons as well as coffee, tea, and mead. Come with an empty stomach, because you'll eat the equivalent of a meal by the time the tour is over. And, Aniruddh promises, you'll also learn a lot about the city, including "the arts, culture, history, the student life—how it all comes together to make Ann Arbor what it is."

(309) 857-2071
bythesidewalk.com

SING THE PRAISES
OF BREAKFAST AT ANGELO'S

Back in the 1980s, singer-songwriter Dick Siegel wrote a song about Angelo's, Ann Arbor's signature breakfast spot. And locals are still enjoying the food! Topping the must-haves on the menu is the house-made bread (white or raisin); it's the key ingredient in Siegel's favorite dish—eggs over easy, hash browns, and toast—as well as the deep-fried French toast smothered with strawberries and blueberries and topped with whipped cream. For lunch, Angelo's offers oodles of options, including four kinds of Reubens, a variety of juicy burgers (three of them meatless), and five club sandwiches. Diehard diners swear by the Angelo's Club, made with savory pork roast and topped with barbecue sauce. Pressed for time? Stop in next door at Angelo's on the Side for a quick coffee or a sandwich to go.

1100 E. Catherine St.
(734) 761-8996
angelosa2.com

TIP
Angelo's is located in the midst of U-M's sprawling medical campus, where finding a place to park can be a challenge. Weekends are a bit easier, with structures available on nearby Glen Avenue and Ann Street.

GO PAN-ASIAN
AT THE PACIFIC RIM

"I'd give this restaurant 20 stars if I could" was one Yelper's overwhelmingly positive review of dining at Pacific Rim, an upscale pan-Asian establishment just around the corner from Main Street. Appetizers and entrees are influenced by Chinese, Japanese, Korean, Thai, and Vietnamese cuisines. And somehow it all works! Customer favorites include sablefish—marinated in miso and sake, then pan roasted, and served over sautéed napa cabbage, shiitake mushrooms, and Korean noodles—as well as five-spice duck and seared bigeye tuna. (The presentation of these dishes is also a feast for the eyes.) To complement your meal, choose from an extensive wine list or try a craft cocktail like Through the Looking Glass, a refreshing blend of lemongrass-infused vodka, sherry, shochu, clementine, lemon, orchard syrup, and celery.

114 W. Liberty St.
(734) 662-9303
pacificrimbykana.com

SINK YOUR TEETH
INTO A MANI OSTERIA PIZZA

You know you've got a good thing going when famous chefs like Bobby Flay come to your business, taste your food, and ask for the recipes. Then the MLive Media Group visits and names one of your dishes the best pizza in Michigan. That's the short history of Mani Osteria, a high-style and family-friendly Italian restaurant with a unique approach to pizza making. The wood-fired ovens create a beautiful, blistered crust. But it's what goes on top that really makes the pizzas pop. Combinations like mozzarella/roasted arugula/bacon/balsamic/chili flakes and forest mushroom/fontina/black truffle/egg are fan favorites. Not in the mood for pizza? Try a small-plate option like cauliflower *fritti* enhanced with shallots, pickled chiles, and bacon jam, or a big-plate entrée like the fire-roasted branzino. *Molto bene*!

341 E. Liberty St.
(734) 769-6700
maniosteria.com

ENJOY PRIME BEEF
AT A2'S CHOP HOUSE

You can do it if you want. You can go into The Chop House and order the roasted rack of venison or blue crab and lobster cakes or tender lamb from Australia. And you'll love it. But the star of the show at this restaurant is beef: the finest USDA prime beef, wet-aged 28 days to flavorful, melt-in-your-mouth perfection and surrounded by equally enjoyable savory side dishes. Take time to enjoy your dinner in the elegant, gas lamp-lit dining room. Then step through an archway into La Dolce Vita, a dessert, liquor, and cigar lounge. It's hard to pick the perfect ending to a perfect meal. But the German chocolate cake with a coconut-pecan crunch and fudge icing, served with malted-milk chocolate gelato, comes very close.

322 S. Main St.
(888) 456-3463
thechophouseannarbor.com

SAMPLE SANDWICHES
FROM ZINGERMAN'S ORIGINAL DELI

In 1982 two friends opened a delicatessen in a small brick building in a quiet near-north neighborhood. Their original offerings included made-to-order sandwiches, Jewish specialties like chopped liver and chicken soup, and buy-by-the-pound meats, cheeses, and smoked fish. Since that time, the deli, named Zingerman's, has grown by leaps and bounds (zounds!) into a food empire with national fame. Besides opening a sit-down restaurant and a Korean café, founders Paul Saginaw and Ari Weinzweig have launched a bakery, a creamery, a candy factory, a coffee company, a mail-order business—even a travel agency taking foodies on tours around the world.

The foundation for all of this, the deli, is still going strong. And it still makes what satisfied customer Barack Obama called "a killer Reuben" among other delicious delights.

Zingerman's Delicatessen
422 Detroit St., (734) 663-3354
zingermansdeli.com

Zingerman's Roadhouse
2501 Jackson Ave., (734) 663-3663
zingermansroadhouse.com

Miss Kim
415 N. Fifth Ave., (734) 275-0099
misskimannarbor.com

FIND YOUR FAVORITE
AT WASHTENAW DAIRY

Visitors to the venerable Washtenaw Dairy, in business since 1934, generally fall into one of two categories. One group comes in to enjoy the huge, hand-dipped ice cream cones. (Singles are equal to competitors' double dips and reasonably priced!) Another group swears by the dairy's mouth-watering donuts. Over a cake donut base, the staff layers vanilla, chocolate, or maple glazes with coconut, sprinkles, or peanut toppings. During football season, you can buy maize-and-blue glazed donuts, and plain donuts rolled in cinnamon sugar are available year-round.

Can't decide between ice cream and donuts? Buy a quart of the former and a dozen of the latter, and create donut-on-the-bottom sundaes to top with your favorite sauce. Hot fudge is highly recommended.

602 S. Ashley St.
(734) 662-3244
washtenawdairy.com

SIP A SANGRIA
AT A TRUE SPANISH RESTAURANT

Let's clear up the confusion right away: Aventura is *not* a tapas bar. It's an upscale Spanish restaurant that serves tapas, including the popular *patatas bravas*, but offers so much more than snack food. The star of its multilayered menu is paella, the national dish of Spain. Choose from six variations of this dish: from Valenciana, featuring bone-in chicken and duck confit, to Verduras, a vegetarian option made of artichokes, green beans, mushrooms, cauliflower, and green onions. Complementing Aventura's food are specially selected wines, beers, and mixed drinks as well as a trio of sangrias that will make you forget that tired old red-wine recipe. Innovative add-ins include cinnamon, fennel, lemongrass, and ginger.

On summer days, grab a seat in the restaurant's courtyard shaded by colorful sails.

216 E. Washington St.
(734) 369-3153
aventuraannarbor.com

BE TRANSPORTED
BY A TEAHAUS BEVERAGE

Looking for a place to watch the world walk by as you slowly sip some tea? The TeaHaus is waiting for you. Enter the storefront at 206 North Fourth Avenue, and choose from more than 175 varieties of loose tea, including black, green, white, fruit, herbal, and rooibos. As your selection steeps, you can pass through the adjoining archway to take a window seat and consider the options on the café menu. Like something sweet? There are mouthwatering macarons. Prefer something more filling? Try the soups, salads, and baguettes.

A traditional English tea experience complete with finger sandwiches and scones can also be prepared at your request. You have Lisa McDonald, a sommelier trained in the tea traditions of Europe, to thank for bringing this bit of Britain to Michigan.

204-206 N. Fourth Ave.
(734) 622-0460
teahaus.com

EXPERIMENT WITH
HOPPY AND SOUR BREWS AT HOMES

Brewpubs abound in Ann Arbor, as do fast-casual Korean restaurants. It was just a matter of time before somebody combined the two, which Tommy Kennedy did in 2017 with HOMES Brewery. But Tommy didn't stop there. He directed his brewmaster to develop the juicy, low-bitterness IPAs he knew most patrons would want, then asked him to add fruity sherbet sours to the menu as well. (One of these, the Blurb sherbet, is described as "a lactose kettle sour made with blueberries and basil" and pours purple!) This eagerness to experiment is one reason HOMES made *USA Today*'s list of the top 10 new breweries. The food has an experimental edge to it, too, with fusion dishes like fries topped with crispy pork, kimchi, red onion, nori, sriracha aioli, and gochujang.

2321 Jackson Ave.
(734) 954-6637
homesbrewery.com

TIP

Don't bother looking for these beers at your local grocery store. Says owner Tommy Kennedy: "The IPAs we're doing don't really lend themselves to being on the shelf for long." You can, however, purchase HOMES's offerings for off-site consumption in growlers and 750 ml. (wine-sized) bottles as well as beer cans and bottles. Just keep the beer cool, and drink it fresh!

DINE INSIDE A DEPOT
AT THE GANDY DANCER RESTAURANT

First you feel the rumble. Then a bell clangs, and everyone starts to clap. It happens every time an Amtrak train passes (very close!) by Gandy Dancer, a depot-turned-restaurant on Ann Arbor's near north side. This 1886 Richardsonian Romanesque structure retains much of its original elegance, making it the city's go-to restaurant for marking milestones in life. But it's the seafood that keeps people coming back, including imaginative interpretations of swordfish and shrimp as well as salmon raised in pristine Antarctic waters. Gandy Dancer is also a popular Sunday brunch site; holiday reservations are highly recommended.

Wondering where the name comes from? It's a slang term for railroad workers who laid and maintained tracks in the days before that work became mechanized.

401 Depot St.
(734) 769-0592
muer.com/gandy-dancer

TAKE A FANCY
TO ANN ARBOR FRAGELS

Ever tried a fragel? It's a raisin bagel that's deep-fried instead of baked, then rolled in cinnamon sugar, and (ideally) served hot. It's the signature snack of this city, and it's impossible to eat just one.

The fragel is the flagship product at MD Bagel Fragel, but it's not the only thing that draws people to this tiny takeout place on the city's far east side across from Arborland Mall. MD's menu also includes 30 traditionally made bagels—including flavors such as cherry almond and spinach feta—and 20 varieties of cream cheese. Decisions, decisions!

Looking for lunchtime fare? Let the staff build you a bagel sandwich; one popular choice layers smoked mozzarella, mayonnaise, pesto, tomato, and red onion.

3500 Washtenaw Ave.
(734) 929-2756
facebook.com/BagelFragel

SHAKE AND STIR
YOUR OWN CRAFT COCKTAILS

You may have heard Tammy Coxen interviewed on Michigan Radio or seen her recent book on Michigan's craft cocktail culture. Why not treat yourself to one of her popular classes and experience firsthand her talent for turning unexpected ingredients into amazing mixed drinks?

Each of Tammy's Tastings includes a bit of history about the topic, instruction on technique, and the chance to mix and enjoy your own cocktails. With more than 50 classes to choose from, you're sure to find something that tickles your tastebuds. Options include Better with Bubbles, Cuban Cocktails, The Manhattan Project, and Winter Warmers. (Favorite title? Pink Drinks that Don't Suck!) Tastings are held around the area; The Last Word, an Ann Arbor cocktail bar, is a frequent venue.

(734) 276-3215
tammystastings.com

KEEP IT MOVING
AT KRAZY JIM'S BLIMPYBURGER

Consistently ranked number one for its burgers, Krazy Jim's Blimpyburger (Blimpy's to locals) is also known for its short-tempered short-order cooks. You can hardly blame them; even though "the rules" for ordering (tell the fry cook if you want any deep-fried sides, then tell the grillmaster how many patties you'd like, then tell the dresser your condiment choices) are displayed on the wall, some newbies try to place their whole order up front. That's when the tongue-lashing begins, all in good fun. Burgers not your thing? Choose from turkey, fish, and chicken sandwiches. Just don't ask for a salad; that'll get the grillmaster going again! Blimpy's formula is simple—good, cheap food made fast—and it works. A fifth generation of customers now frequents the place.

304 S. Ashley St.
(734) 663-4590
blimpyburger.com

2

DRINK UP
AT A POPULAR TOWNIE TAVERN

This city has hundreds of dining establishments to choose from and its fair share of chain restaurants and bars. But if you really want to experience the Ann Arbor "vibe," venture out to a neighborhood tavern and belly up to the bar.

Serving the southeast side is Banfield's Bar and Grill, tucked into a Packard Road strip mall. Stiff drinks, a savory fish fry, and Saturday morning breakfasts top the menu, and can be served around an interior fire pit.

3140 Packard Rd.
(734) 971-3300
banfieldsbar.com

Further up Packard is Fraser's Pub. Fraser's tots served with Muenster cheese, bacon, onion, tomato, salsa, and sour cream are a fan favorite, as is the slow-roasted pulled-pork sandwich. Patio and picnic-table seating are available.

2045 Packard Rd.
(734) 665-1955
fraserspub.com

26

Casey's Tavern is the choice of northsiders. Weekly specials include one pasta, one Mexican dish, and another that is chef's choice. The popular Salmwich features flaked, roasted salmon with scallions, peppers, goat cheese, tomato, and red onion.

304 Depot St.
(734) 665-6775
caseys-tavern.com

Old Town Tavern, located in a downtown building that has been a watering hole since 1898, is a west-side favorite for its strong southwestern menu. Live folk and jazz music can be heard here on Wednesdays and Sundays.

122 W. Liberty St.
(734) 662-9291
oldtownaa.com

TIP

It's *not* a tavern. But Knight's, a casual fine-dining establishment near Veterans Memorial Park, is definitely a townie hangout. Weekend evenings are usually packed to the rafters with folks looking for a great steak from the Knight family's own butcher shop and a strong drink. (#StrongDrinks is even their Twitter hashtag!) Daily dinner promotions like Roasted Turkey Tuesdays and Pot Roast Wednesdays draw regulars in even more frequently.

2324 Dexter Ave.
(734) 665-8644
knightsrestaurants.com

MAKE THE MOST
OF THE MEAT MENU AT BIERCAMP

Biercamp bills itself as a meat shop, but that's like calling the Mona Lisa a pretty good painting. Owners Walt Hansen and Hanna Cheadle are artists who happen to work in the butcher business, offering up a dozen kinds of sausage—including a vegetarian version—which they grind and stuff on site. They also slow smoke meats (behold the 12-hour brisket!) and have elevated jerky to a new level with flavors like Jamaican jerk pork, sriracha chicken, and Korean barbecue turkey. Any of this can be wrapped to go, enjoyed inside, or taken out front to the streetside beer garden.

True to its name, Biercamp is also a microbrewery, rotating through more than 20 varieties made in small batches to ensure the freshest taste. House-made root beer is available for under-agers.

1643 S. State St.
(734) 995-2437
bier-camp.com

RELAX WITH
A MEAD-Y PINT AT BLØM MEADWORKS

If the only time you've tasted mead, a fermented honey wine, was at a Renaissance fair, you're in for a big surprise. Bløm Meadworks approaches mead as a craft brewer approaches beer: with the goal of making it light, dry, carbonated, and remarkably "sessionable." (That means the alcohol content is low enough for someone to enjoy several pints in a single sitting.) The fermentation process leaves lots of room for creativity; some of Bløm's most popular add-ins include apples and berries, seasonal spices, hops, even hints of distilled spirits. Pair your favorite with a cheese or chocolate board for a light snack, or bring in your own food; the owners don't mind. The atmosphere here is very relaxed, with evening trivia and board-game gatherings plus Sunday-afternoon yoga filling the calendar of this business's community-building efforts.

100 S. Fourth Ave.
(734) 548-9729
drinkblom.com

SATISFY A CRAVING
FOR CAFFEINE AT SWEETWATERS

In 1993, Wei and Lisa Bee opened a business in Ann Arbor to provide "globally influenced coffees and teas in an environment that is both classic and friendly." The concept caught on quickly, enabling them to branch out into other parts of Michigan and 11 other states.

One reason for their popularity is that customers clamor for their coffee creations such as French Vietnamese au Lait, featuring dark-roasted chicory coffee mixed with sweetened condensed milk. Their trademark Ice Dragons are creamy frozen beverages built upon a base of coffee or fruit. And they even make shakes with coffee, like the Napali Brew that blends vanilla ice cream with espresso and hazelnut syrup. A line of Sweetwaters specialty teas, as well as a menu of pastries and desserts, rounds out their offerings.

sweetwaterscafe.com

SWEETWATERS LOCATIONS

Downtown
123 W. Washington St.
(734) 769-2331

Kerrytown
407 N. Fifth Ave.
(734) 622-0084

Meijer
3145 Ann Arbor-Saline Rd.
(734) 369-8697

Plymouth Green
3393 Plymouth Rd.
(734) 369-4568

U-M Liberty
604 E. Liberty St.
(734) 929-2398

U-M Michigan Union
530 S. State St.
(734) 548-8088

Westgate
(inside the Ann Arbor District Library)
2503 Jackson Ave.
(734) 827-5116

REACH NEW HEIGHTS
WITH THE FOOD AT EVEREST SHERPA

How do you describe the food at Everest Sherpa? With influences from the cultures of Nepal, India, and Tibet, Himalayan fusion might be your best bet. Owned by a family native to south Asia, this restaurant offers simple but classic favorites ranging from *momos* (dumplings) on the appetizer list to curry, masala, and *makhani* entrées. (Not sure what you want? Come first for the lunch buffet, and sample your way through.) This is an easy place to work around dietary restrictions, as many dishes are vegetarian and most others can be made that way. Gluten-free options are also included. Everest Sherpa has a full bar, but the nonalcoholic mango lassi (a fruit-and-yogurt smoothie) complements most any meal.

2803 Oak Valley Dr.
(734) 997-5490
everestsherparestaurant.com

HEAP ON THE HASH
AT FLEETWOOD DINER

To paraphrase Arlo Guthrie, you can get anything you want at this Ann Arbor restaurant: eggs, breakfast meat, pancakes, etc. But what you've got to get from the Fleetwood, at least once, is a dish called Hippie Hash. It starts with a base of crispy hash browns that gets piled high with grilled green peppers, onions, tomatoes, broccoli, and mushrooms. The finish? A generous sprinkling of feta cheese. This is the item that propelled the Fleetwood to a place among Thrillist's best 24-hour diners in America. But the atmosphere played a part, too. Inside the building—made from a 1940s diner kit—is a counter full of barstools giving you a grill-side seat to the making of your meal. Outside, an awning shades tables that are the perfect platform for people-watching.

300 S. Ashley St.
(734) 995-5502
thefleetwooddiner.com

MUSIC AND ENTERTAINMENT

GROOVE ON
AT THE JAZZY BLUE LLAMA

Cool cats agree: the Blue LLama Jazz Club is a local gem. Musician Dave Sharp serves as artistic director for the club, arranging for acts that run the gamut from straight-ahead to contemporary experimental to genre-crossing artists. And the space is intimate, seating only 100 people—so wherever you end up, you'll have a great view. But that's not all. The two capital Ls in the club's name are not a typo; they represent management's "Love of music *and* Love of food." The menus, developed by executive chef (and musician) Louis Goral, are made up of jazz-inspired shared plates, like the crispy foie gras PB&J—a play on Lady Day's favorite snack.

Rising artists perform Sundays from 11:30 a.m. to 2:30 p.m. during the Blue LLama's jazz brunch.

314 S. Main St.
(734) 373-3300

TIP
Each September, the Blue LLama plays host to the Ann Arbor Jazz Festival, a free three-day event featuring professional Michigan musicians as well as student performances and workshops.

FIND YOUR FOLK
UPSTAIRS AT THE ARK

If you like live music that tells a story, you'll love The Ark—Ann Arbor's nationally known venue for folk, roots, and ethnic music. Established in 1965, The Ark has hosted many musical greats over the years and makes a point of inviting them back throughout their careers. This means that one week you may encounter the legendary Richard Thompson on stage and the next be tapping your toes to Rhiannon Giddens and the Carolina Chocolate Drops. The Ark's staff books more than 300 performances a year, enabling you to easily find your favorites.

For a more concentrated musical experience, check out the Ann Arbor Folk Festival. This January event, showcasing the talents of a dozen acts at U-M's Hill Auditorium, is a fundraiser organized by and for The Ark.

316 S. Main St.
(734) 761-1800
theark.org

LISTEN UP
AT TWO TOWER(ING) CARILLONS

Of the 600-some carillons in the world, the University of Michigan has not one but two for you to enjoy. (A quick primer: A carillon is a set of enormous bells controlled by a keyboard of wooden levers and foot pedals that are played with the fists—yes, fists!—and the feet, respectively.) The first, the Charles Baird Carillon, was unveiled in 1936 in Burton Memorial Tower on Central Campus. The newest, the Ann and Robert H. Lurie Carillon, debuted in 1996 on North Campus. Faculty, staff, and students give regular performances on both of these instruments. Selections are at the discretion of the musicians; on a given day, you might hear anything from the *Star Wars* theme to a Scarlatti sonata.

Charles Baird Carillon
smtd.umich.edu/about/facilities/burton-memorial-tower/charles-baird-carillon

Ann and Robert H. Lurie Carillon
smtd.umich.edu/about/facilities/lurie-carillon

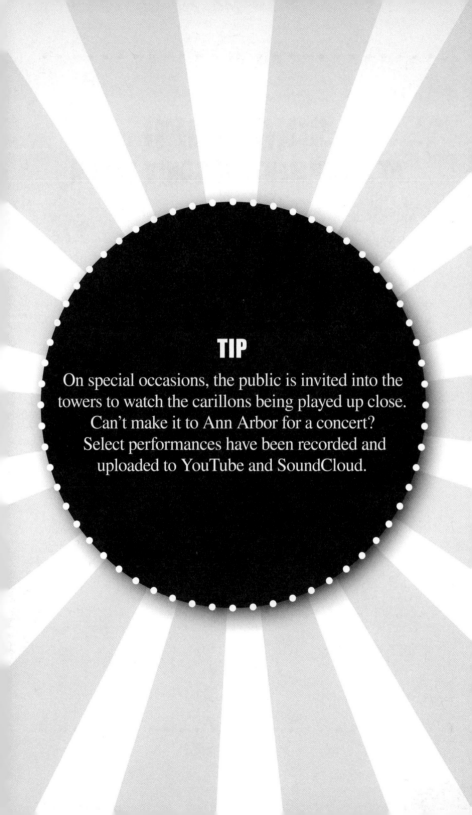

TIP

On special occasions, the public is invited into the towers to watch the carillons being played up close. Can't make it to Ann Arbor for a concert? Select performances have been recorded and uploaded to YouTube and SoundCloud.

SING ALONG
AT A SUMMERTIME SONIC LUNCH

If you're walking downtown and hear the amplified opening notes of a rock ballad, you're probably close to Liberty Plaza: site of the Sonic Lunch concert series, held Thursdays from June through August. Relax on the plaza's benches, and experience a wide range of talent running the gamut from blues, country, and indie rock to Motown magic. And the organizers sometimes book talent from the NBC show *The Voice* for good measure. You're welcome to bring in food and drink, or purchase a meal from local vendors set up on site. The best perk of all? The concerts, sponsored by the Bank of Ann Arbor, are free. Starting time is 11:30 a.m., but it's advisable to get there early for your pick of seating.

Corner of Liberty and Division Sts. (Liberty Plaza)
(734) 662-1600
soniclunch.com

BOOT-SCOOT
YOUR WAY TO NASHBASH

For a taste of country in the middle of the city, nothing beats Nashbash Music Festival. This outdoor festival, held the third Thursday in August, sets up in the Ann Arbor Farmers Market space and has a down-home feel to it. The Kerrytown Merchants Association brings in real Nashville talent to perform alongside local country stars. You're encouraged to sing along if you know the songs and to two-step if the spirit moves you! Everybody's here to have a good time, so don't worry about being judged. (Locals never do!)

Bring a picnic basket, or patronize the vendors serving beer, wine, soft drinks, and food—including mouth-watering barbecue. After 10 p.m., an after-party kicks in across Fourth Avenue in the Braun Court courtyard.

315 Detroit St. (Ann Arbor Farmers Market)
Kerrytown.org

SPEND WEEKS
ENJOYING THE SUMMER FESTIVAL

For three weeks each year, Ann Arbor becomes the entertainment capital of Michigan. And that's no exaggeration! Each day at the Ann Arbor Summer Festival, there are at least half a dozen events to choose from. Some, like dance performances, major musical acts, and comedy shows, are ticketed and staged indoors at venues across the city. Others—free concerts, movies by moonlight, and acrobatic spectacles—are held along Ingalls Mall, a beautiful campus courtyard with U-M's Rackham Hall as a backdrop.

At the other end is a section of the festival called The Annex, where you can create art, compete in a trivia contest, or talk with the talent from U-M's public radio station. Two other things to keep you occupied: a kid zone and a beer garden. 'Nuff said?

915 E. Washington St.
(734) 995-5999
a2sf.org

TIP

Planning to visit Ann Arbor during the school year? Consult the calendar of the University Musical Society. UMS arranges more than 70 music, theater, and dance performances by professional touring artists each season and hosts over 100 free educational activities for residents and visitors alike.

(734) 764-2538
ums.org

SWING AND SWAY
AT AN OUTDOOR DANCE FESTIVAL

"Calling out around the world, are you ready for a brand-new beat? Summer's here and the time is right"—for the Dancing in the Streets festival!

Held downtown on the first Sunday in September, DITS gives you a chance to sample dance traditions from different times in history *and* different parts of the world, using Main and Washington Streets as your dance floor. In past years, attendees have been treated to lessons in everything from swing and salsa to the hora and the hula. Musicians accompany the dancers and provide mini-concerts for all to enjoy. The Ann Arbor Community for Traditional Music and Dance organizes this free event, which includes activities for children including a maypole and a musical instrument "petting zoo."

Corner of Main and Washington Sts.
aactmad.org/dits

GET APRIL FOOLISH
AT THE FESTIFOOLS PARADE

Some people will take advantage of any opportunity to dress up and have fun. If you're one of those people, or one who enjoys watching others get silly, you'll get a kick out of the FestiFOOLs parade. Held in the afternoon of the first Sunday in April to celebrate the coming of spring, this parade is a public art spectacular featuring crazy, colorful papier-mâché puppets created by U-M students with the help of community volunteers. The puppets are larger than life—think Chinatown dragon-sized!—and hoisted aloft by handlers so that all can see them.

A related event, FOOLMoon, is held the evening of the prior Friday at the nearby Ann Arbor Farmers Market. Music, dancing, laser shows, and luminaries mark this all-ages entertainment.

Main St. between Washington and William Sts.
(734) 763-7550
wonderfoolproductions.org

SEE THE BEST
AT THE CINETOPIA FILM FEST

Imagine an event that brings together the best of famous film festivals like Sundance, SXSW, Tribeca, Toronto, Cannes, Berlin, and more for you to explore and enjoy. That's the concept behind Cinetopia. Over the course of 10 days in May, you can view more than 60 narrative and documentary films at a dozen venues in southeast Michigan, including Ann Arbor's Michigan Theater and State Theater and U-M's Angell Hall. What's more, filmmakers and industry experts also appear to headline events like panels and Q&A sessions. Want to avoid the crowds? Buy Cinetopia tickets in advance for individual screenings or blocks of screenings, or VIP passes that give you access to reserve seating, pre- and post-festival parties, and meet-and-greets.

603 E. Liberty St. (Michigan Theater)
(734) 668-8397
cinetopiafestival.org

SETTLE IN
FOR A COLLAGE OF PERFORMANCES

One minute, you're listening raptly to a theater soliloquy. Then, across the stage, a spotlight captures a trombone ensemble interpreting a Shostakovich prelude, followed by a snippet of dance set to the music of the movie *Beasts of the Southern Wild.*

What you're witnessing is the aptly titled Collage Concert of U-M's School of Music, Theatre & Dance. Created in 1977 as entertainment for a music conference, Collage has since become a signature event of the SMTD winter season. The event's design is unique, featuring all the ensembles and departments of the school performing one arresting work after another. It's an evening of bravura performances at breakneck speed, presented each year in January at the university's historic Hill Auditorium.

825 N. University Ave. (Hill Auditorium)
(734) 764-2538
smtd.umich.edu/performances-events

FALL IN LOVE
WITH THE HISTORIC MICHIGAN THEATER

It's hard to believe that the Michigan Theater, Ann Arbor's iconic movie palace built in the 1920s, was once slated for demolition. Now it's the unofficial cultural center of the community—still hosting movies but also providing a home for the local symphony and a performance space for touring musical acts, stage productions, comedy shows, lectures, and more.

The main auditorium, seating 1,610, is adorned with elegant Romanesque arches highlighted with gold leaf. Within this striking space is a lovingly restored Barton pipe organ, which rises from beneath the stage to be played before movies and big events. (A calendar of performances can be found on the website.) Another plus? The concessionaires serve beer and wine *and* proudly pump real butter on your popcorn!

603 E. Liberty St.
(734) 668-8397
michtheater.org

TIP

The Michigan Theater also hosts the Ann Arbor Film Festival, the oldest avant-garde and experimental film competition in North America. Over the years, thousands of influential filmmakers have exhibited their early work at AAFF, including George Lucas, Yoko Ono, and Gus Van Sant. The festival, typically held in March, is a six-day event, and no two evenings are the same. In between screenings, you'll be treated to creative programming like filmmaker interviews, gallery installations, and panel discussions.

(734) 995-9356
aafilmfest.org

SIT OUTSIDE
AND ENJOY A PENNY SEATS PLAY

There's no shortage of good theatre in Washtenaw County, but one company sees its mission a little differently than the others. As the Penny Seats website says, "We think theatre should be fun and stirring. We believe going to a show should not break the bank. And we find Michigan summer evenings beautiful." To that end, this group of energetic artists presents the summer segment of their schedule in a bandshell amid the grassy surroundings of Ann Arbor's West Park. Bring a blanket or a lawn chair and a basket of snacks to enjoy a full range of dramas, comedies, and musicals—both classic and new—for the price of a movie ticket. Foul-weather productions are staged at the Stone Chalet Bed and Breakfast Inn and Event Center.

215 Chapin St. (West Park)
(734) 926-5346
pennyseats.org

ENJOY IMPROV
AND A PINT AT POINTLESS BREWERY

In an unassuming strip mall on the southeast side of town, comic actors scream, cry, fake-faint, fall to the ground, and anything else they can think of to spin a story and make an audience laugh. That's the essence of what you'll find at Pointless Brewery & Theatre, Ann Arbor's home of professional improvisational humor. Every show is made up on the spot, often prompted by verbal cues from the audience. What follows is as unexpected for the performers as it is for everyone else—and that's the great fun of it! In between guffaws, you can grab a pint of Pointless's half-dozen specialty beers, all brewed on site. Anybody for a chocolate peanut butter milkshake stout? (Yes, that's a real concoction!)

3014 Packard St.
(989) 455-4484
pointlessbrew.com

BE AMUSED
BY GILBERT & SULLIVAN

"It is a glorious thing, to be a pirate king" . . . or to watch an actor portray one in a University of Michigan Gilbert & Sullivan Society production. UMGASS was founded in 1947, and is the country's oldest student-run society dedicated to performing the comic operas of Sir William Gilbert and Sir Arthur Sullivan. Each year the society invites community members to collaborate on several fully staged productions of Gilbert and Sullivan operettas, which are then performed with an orchestra at the Lydia Mendelssohn Theatre inside the Michigan League. Though the quality of the productions sets a high standard for community G&S companies, the tickets are surprisingly affordable. Join in the tradition of singing "God Save the Queen" (don't worry; the words are in the playbill) at the beginning of every performance!

911 N. University Ave. (Michigan League)
(734) 647-8436
umgass.org

SIT UP CLOSE
AT THE KERRYTOWN CONCERT HOUSE

At a recent concert at the Kerrytown Concert House, Brazilian mandolinist and composer Danilo Brito told the audience that "playing here is like playing for you in my own living room." That's because this unique performance space has been carved out of a real 19th-century residence, giving it a close-up feeling not found in more traditional venues.

But size doesn't stop the concert house from hosting hundreds of musical events each year—including everything from national and international artists to emerging talent living in the local area. Imagine a chamber music quartet one night, a "wine, women, and song" cabaret another night, and a performer of world music—like Brito—on a third. KCH also promotes daring directions in music with its four-day Edgefest celebration, held in October.

415 N. Fourth Ave.
(734) 769-2999
kerrytownconcerthouse.com

SPORTS AND RECREATION

CHEER ON
A2'S SEMI-PRO SOCCER TEAMS

"COY-MO! COY-MO! Come on, you Mighty Oak!" That's a chant you'll likely hear if you pass by Concordia University's football field on a summer night. Mighty Oak is a nickname for AFC Ann Arbor, a soccer club that prepares elite college athletes and other amateurs for the big leagues. As of this printing, 18 players had pushed on to become pros—an impressive record for a club that's only been around since 2014. In 2018, the club organized a women's semi-pro side that's also making a splash in soccer circles. Both teams play at home at Concordia from May through July. If you get really enthused, you can join their diehard fan club: the Main Street Hooligans. Info about that—and the words to all their songs and chants—is available at mainstreethooligans.com.

4090 Geddes Rd. (Concordia University football field)
(734) 408-1627
afcannarbor.com

BAKE BESIDE
THE EXPERTS AT ZINGERMAN'S

If you've ever enjoyed the tender crumb of a Zingerman's brioche or the cinn-ful aroma of their cinnamon rolls, imagine this: being able to prepare these baked goods all on your own. That's the idea behind BAKE!—Zingerman's hands-on teaching bakery.

At the BAKE! facility in south Ann Arbor, staffers share their knowledge and love of food with the home-baker community through dozens of bread-, pastry-, pie-, and cake-making classes, including some just for kids and families. If you really want to enhance your skills, you can sign up for a BAKE!-cation: a two-day workshop that takes a deep dive into a broad category of baking. Whatever you choose, you'll leave the bakery with the food you made in class and the inspiration, skills, and recipes to do it again at home.

3723 Plaza Dr.
(734) 761-7255
bakewithzing.com

PEDAL OR PACK
ACROSS THE BORDER-TO-BORDER TRAIL

Ready to get off the road and experience the *real* Washtenaw County? The east-west Border-to-Border Trail (B2B) was made for you. This paved pathway, mostly hugging the Huron River, will connect you to extraordinary views of water, woods, and wildlife all along its length. You can enter the path at eight trailheads. No motorized vehicles are allowed (except mobility vehicles), but you can walk, bike, and blade with abandon. Comfort stations are available in parks, and bike repair spots are thoughtfully placed along the way. Fun fact: B2B is part of the Iron Belle Trail, a 2,000-mile network of paths that links Ironwood, Michigan, in the western Upper Peninsula with Detroit's Belle Isle Park in the southeast Lower Peninsula. Ride on!

washtenaw.org/334/Border-to-Border-Trail

TIP

You'll pass by or through more than 20 parks and nature areas on the Washtenaw County B2B. New segments are added regularly; check the website for updated maps.

DROP IN FOR A SPIN
AT THE SKATE PARK

A clover bowl. A 10-foot right kidney bowl with pool coping and stairs. Flow bowls and a spine, a crooked ditch, big and small hubbas, three sets of stairs and rails, a straight rail, hips, quarter pipes, and skateable boulders. If these terms resonate with you, then grab a board and get going to the Ann Arbor Skate Park. Located at the northwestern corner of Veterans Memorial Park, this skateboarding facility provides a safe but challenging environment for adults and kids interested in perfecting their skills. For easy access, the park is open from 6 a.m. to 10 p.m. year-round and has no admission fee. One of the local hospitals operates an urgent care clinic across the street just in case you take a tumble!

350 N. Maple Rd.
(734) 794-6445
a2skatepark.org

ROOT, ROOT, ROOT
FOR THE ROLLER DERBY DIMES

In winter, Buhr Park's open-air arena plays host to ice skaters practicing their spins and chassés. In the summer, an entirely different set of skaters steps in to take over: the Ann Arbor Derby Dimes. These local roller derby stars have adopted funny names for themselves, like Hellinor Bruisevelt and Little Awful Annie. But they compete seriously in their sport—much to the roaring pleasure of their fans. You can cheer them on, too, as they hip-whip and wall-out their opponents, sometimes getting "rink rash" for their efforts! Check their schedule for home bouts in May, June, July, and August. Soft drinks and snacks are available, with locally brewed beer and cider for guests 21 and over.

2751 Packard Rd. (Buhr Park ice arena)
a2derbydimes.org

RIDE THE RAPIDS
OF THE ARGO PARK CASCADES

Years ago, planners had the foresight to set aside park lands along the scenic Huron River, which winds its way through the city. But they really outdid themselves in 2012, when they established the Argo Park Cascades. Carved out of the spillway around an old dam, the Cascades provide tubers, rafters, and kayakers with a class II whitewater experience. (For novices, that means easy rapids with small waves and wide channels.) Between the rapids are quiet pools of shallow water; so if you get tipped out, you can easily get back in. To be on the safe side, life preservers are recommended for little ones.

It takes about 30 minutes to complete the trip and just five to pick up your watercraft and walk back to the start. How many trips can *you* make in one visit?

1055 Longshore Dr.
(734) 794-6241
a2gov.org/departments/Parks-Recreation/parks-places/argo

TIP
Argo Park is busy on nice-weather weekends, and parking is limited. Overflow spaces are available at 416 Longshore Drive as well as at U-M's Kellogg Eye Center at 900 Wall Street.

TIP

The Cascades are just one part of the Huron River Water Trail, a 104-mile inland waterway connecting people with nature from western Oakland County to the river's mouth at Lake Erie. Visit Milford, Dexter, Ann Arbor, Ypsilanti, and Flat Rock, and enjoy fishing and a variety of paddle sports as you make your way along. This Huron River resource has been designated a National Water Trail, thanks to its primary sponsors: the Huron River Watershed Council and the River Up! initiative.

huronriverwatertrail.org

DO THE ZOO
AT CREATURE CONSERVANCY

Lions and tigers and bears? Try warthogs, tortoises, and African porcupines—including one named Bedhead—as well as North American cougars and bald eagles. These are among the 80 species you'll find at the Creature Conservancy, a sanctuary that houses both rescue animals and transplants with the goal of advancing conservation through education. Though many enclosures are outside, the heart of the facility is the education building, where you can experience the animals up close during curator talks. For events like October's Spooky Species, even more animals are brought in by special arrangement with the Columbus Zoo. Creature Conservancy also does its part to preserve threatened species, like South American sloths, through captive breeding programs. Look for them in the rafters!

4950 Ann Arbor-Saline Rd.
(734) 929-9324
thecreatureconservancy.org

TIP

Fond of furry creatures? Then make time to visit two other sites in Ann Arbor, both located at the sprawling office building complex called Domino's Farms. On the north side of Domino's is The Petting Farm, where domesticated barnyard animals eagerly await your visit. On the west side is a pasture that sustains a private herd of bison. For your protection, absolutely no petting is allowed at the latter.

3001 Earhart Rd.
(734) 998-0182
pettingfarm.com

SAY AHHHH! TO AI CHI
IN WCC'S WARM POOL

There are gyms with exercise equipment, and a few full-service fitness centers also have lap pools. But there's only one place in Ann Arbor that can boast a warm-saltwater pool for relaxation and rehabilitation: the Health & Fitness Center at Washtenaw Community College. Admission to the center is generally limited to members, but visitors can purchase a one-day, one-week, or one-month pass. With any of those, you'll be welcome to use the warm pool—where you can enjoy ai chi classes (water-based tai chi)—and other amenities including a lap pool, hot tubs, an equipment room, a yoga studio, an indoor walking track, and an outdoor platform tennis court. A café with healthy sips and snacks is an extra perk.

4833 E. Huron River Dr.
(734) 975-9950
wccfitness.org

CHALLENGE YOUR KIDS
TO A FUN ROUND OF FOOTGOLF

It sounds kind of crazy, but there's actually a sport that combines soccer with golf. Called FootGolf, you play it on a regular golf course according to regular golf rules—but using your foot instead of a club to propel the ball. Your challenge is to get the (#5 soccer) ball into the (21-inch) cup with as few strokes (kicks) as possible.

The city of Ann Arbor has set up an 18-hole FootGolf course for you to try at its Huron Hills Golf Course. Holes range from 45 to 219 yards in length, making it easy for most any age to play. To preserve the greens, course management prohibits cleats; indoor soccer or turf shoes are recommended instead. Insider tip: Experienced FootGolfers enhance their outfits with colorful knee-high argyle socks!

3465 E. Huron River Dr. (Huron Hills Golf Course)
(734) 794-6246
a2gov.org/departments/Parks-Recreation/play/Pages/FootGolf.aspx

GET STEAMY
AT MATTHAEI BOTANICAL GARDENS

No time for a Caribbean cruise? Visit U-M's Matthaei Botanical Gardens instead, and enjoy the steamy warmth of the tropics in the glass-enclosed conservatory. Botanical specimens from around the world reach up to the ceiling and down to the floor, surrounding you in a leafy embrace. Plants from temperate and arid environments are also here to be enjoyed. Like to take something home for your garden? Cuttings from flowers in the temperate zone are nurtured in the greenhouse and transplanted into containers for purchase at the annual Mother's Day sale.

In good weather, multiple outdoor gardens await, including one focused on medicinal plants. Bring your walking shoes to take advantage of the four-seasons trails that wind through woods and over water; one trail encircling Willow Pond has been made universally accessible for all to enjoy.

1800 N. Dixboro Rd.
(734) 647-7600
mbgna.umich.edu/matthaei-botanical-gardens

DO SOME DIY
AT THE MICHIGAN FOLK SCHOOL

Talk about hands on! The classes offered by the Michigan Folk School—a center for teaching traditional folk arts, crafts, and skills—are the ultimate do-it-yourself experience, with experts guiding you along every step of the way. Want to handle a hammer and tongs? Take a blacksmithing course and sign your kids up, too. Fascinated by the fascinators worn in recent royal weddings? Learn the fine art of hat making (millinery). Have a hankering for honey? Beekeeping is another ancient art that MFS experts can impart. Choose from more than 30 classes a session, most of them held in a quiet rural setting called Staebler Farm County Park, established to "foster sustainable, healthy living and celebrate the rich farming traditions of Washtenaw County."

7734 Plymouth Rd. (Staebler Farm County Park)
(734) 985-0198
mifolkschool.com

GET YOUR GAME ON
WITH MICHIGAN FOOTBALL

What's it like to be at a U-M football game? In a word, *electric*! It starts with the tradition of welcoming the marching band into the nation's largest stadium—seating over 107,000—and witnessing a dramatic drumline performance. Then the team bursts out of a tunnel and touches an M Go Blue banner as they run out onto the field. With each U-M score, cheerleaders do backflips off the brick wall, and spontaneous renditions of The Wave ripple around the bowl. The halftime show is a huge crowd-pleaser (think themes like *Game of Thrones*, superheroes, and Motown). Then it's back to the game, from which the Wolverines—America's winningest team— usually emerge victorious. A stop at the M Den to pick up Michigan merchandise is the icing on the cake for this game-day experience!

1201 S. Main St.

mgoblue.com/sports/2017/6/16/facilities-michigan-stadium-html

TIP
Michigan Stadium is not open to the public for exercising, walk-in tours, or drop-by photo ops. However, for a fee, you can arrange for a weekday guided tour through U-M's Special Events office at (734) 764-4599.

TIP

Before the game, set aside an hour to immerse yourself in U-M football history at the Towsley Family Museum located inside Schembechler Hall. Showstopping displays include a "win wall" of over 900 footballs marking every Wolverine victory; Harmon Corner, honoring one of Michigan's most accomplished QBs; and the half-dozen jerseys the program has retired.

1200 State St.
(734) 647-4310
mgoblue.com/sports/2017/6/16/fanzone-towsley-museum-html

STOP AND SMELL
THE PEONIES AT NICHOLS ARBORETUM

Fond of scented flowers? Don't miss the largest collection of heirloom peonies in North America, blooming from late May to mid-June in U-M's Nichols Arboretum (AKA The Arb). The Peony Garden was a gift from W. E. Upjohn of pharmaceutical fame, who donated cuttings from his own estate to establish this rare resource in 1922. Stroll through the beds on a self-guided tour, and bring a picnic to enjoy along the edges. If you have time and would enjoy the walk, follow the nearby path that meanders 50 feet down to the Huron River. Along the way, you can veer off to visit wooded tracts, a prairie, a glen of glacial boulders—even a magnolia grove. (Yes, some magnolias varieties *do* grow this far north!)

1610 Washington Hts.
(734) 647-7600
mbgna.umich.edu/nichols-arboretum

TIP

If you visit the peonies in early evening, you'll be perfectly positioned to enjoy Shakespeare in The Arb. This annual production, staged throughout the arboretum in June to take advantage of its dramatic landscape, stars local actors and students from U-M's Residential College.

1610 Washington Hts. (Nichols Arboretum)
(734) 763-0032
lsa.umich.edu/rc/programs-and-community-engagement/
shakespeare-in-the-arb

FLEX YOUR FINGERS
AT PINBALL PETE'S

Remember when you were young and saved up all your quarters for a trip to the local arcade? You can recreate that experience at Pinball Pete's, located in the Galleria Mall in the heart of the student shopping district. Prepare to be wowed as you step down the stairs and see a 10,000-square-foot gaming space unfold before you. Electronic skee-ball and basketball are here with Donkey Kong and Frogger, Tetris, Galaga, and Guitar Hero, too. Impress the crowd (or not!) with your Dance Dance Revolution moves and Daytona driving skills. And, of course, you can play pinball to your heart's content, with dozens of machines at the ready. More adult pursuits, like pool and air hockey, are included in the mix, but Pete's is definitely a family-friendly place. Bring your kids!

1214 S. University Ave.
(734) 213-2502
pinballpetes.org

GO LATIN
WITH FRIENDS AT DANCE REVOLUTION

¡Viva la revolución! The Dance Revolution, that is: Ann Arbor's go-to studio to learn Latin dances like those featured on *Dancing with the Stars*—including salsa, mambo, merengue, and cha-cha—without the snarky judges' comments. The studio is the passion project of Laura Geldys, who has made it her mission to introduce this performing art form to anyone who's game to try it.

Laura and her colleagues offer drop-in lessons on Wednesday, Thursday, and Saturday evenings and dance parties the first and third Saturdays of each month. No partner is required, and no experience is necessary (though private lessons are available if you'd like to get a "leg up"). Just bring some smooth-soled shoes, and prepare to work up *el sudor*!

220 S. Main St. (Phoenix Center)
(313) 808-0358
a2dancerevolution.com

STRETCH YOUR QUADS
AT THE ANN ARBOR GODDESS RUN

Ann Arbor has a long history with road races, supporting a marathon and half marathon as well as dozens of short-distance runs over the years. But only one focuses on women and serves as a fundraiser for charities that benefit women: the Ann Arbor Goddess Run. Start by picking from four events: a 10K, 5K, one-mile fun run, and the Iron Goddess (a combination of the 10K and 5K). Then come up with a costume; colorful tutus are the norm. Special awards are given to groups of females—mothers and daughters, three generations of women, and teams—who run in the same event. In addition to T-shirts, swag includes what organizers describe as "big, giant, blingy finishers' medals"! A post-race brunch is provided for all finishers.

epicraces.com/events/suburban-chevrolet-ann-arbor-goddess-5k

YELL LIKE HELL
AT A U-M YOST HOCKEY GAME

U-M has its share of state-of-the-art athletic facilities, with luxury locker rooms and conditioning equipment that rival the pros. But there's something to be said for doing it old-school, too: an experience that players and fans share at Yost Ice Arena. Opened in 1923, Yost has at various times served the track, basketball, baseball, and football teams. In 1973, it transitioned into a hockey venue and never looked back. Seating around 6,000, the arena is a fan favorite and an opponent's nightmare for the same reason: You're so close to the action. The student section is loud and proud; be prepared for some choice chants and entertaining antics, like telling the opposing goalie he's ugly every time he takes off his mask. Free skating for ticket holders after each game!

1116 S. State St.
(734) 764-4600
mgoblue.com/sports/2017/6/16/facilities-yost-arena-html

TIP
Even after recent renovations, most of the seating at Yost is made up of backless aluminum bleachers. Bring a stadium cushion for maximum comfort.

CULTURE AND HISTORY

JOIN A2 MODERN
ON A MID-CENTURY HOME TOUR

Take a drive up Washtenaw Avenue after it splits with Stadium Boulevard, and what do you see? An impressive array of late 19th- and early 20th-century mansions that are exemplars of their styles. But Ann Arbor's architectural wonders don't stop there. Just blocks away is one of several neighborhoods that are favorites for fans of the mid-century modernist movement.

Modernist architects including George Brigham, James Livingston, Robert Metcalf, and David Osler designed homes for many residents of Ann Arbor Hills and Barton Hills, making use of expansive windows and open floor plans to give the illusion of bringing the outside in. Want to walk through one of their masterpieces? Watch the website of a group called A2 Modern for news of upcoming tours, open houses, lectures, and other activities.

a2modern.org

PLEASE TOUCH
EVERYTHING AT THE HANDS-ON MUSEUM

Traveling with children and looking for an activity that will entertain them for hours? Stop by the Ann Arbor Hands-On Museum. AAHOM is filled with fun exhibits focused on the STEM subjects—science, technology, engineering, and math—and the natural world. And the emphasis is on interactivity; there are no limits to what kids can touch. Preschoolers will love the water tables (bring a change of clothing for them!) and giant building blocks. Older kids can manipulate magnets, build bubbles around themselves, or play a stringless laser harp. Other exhibits focus on light, optics, and visual effects. Predictably, the building can get a bit loud with all this activity. If your child needs a quieter, more sensory-friendly environment, ask for a special kit that includes fidgets, headphones, and sunglasses.

220 E. Ann St.
(734) 995-5439
aahom.org

TIP
On Thursday nights, the museum stays open late and offers a "$5 after 5" deal, less than half the usual cost of admission.

VISIT FOUR ART FAIRS
IN ONE WEEKEND

July is a hot time in Ann Arbor in more ways than one. As one major event, the Ann Arbor Summer Festival, winds down, another begins: the city's famous art fair weekend. During this time, thousands of people arrive to scour the streets in search of some of the best paintings, photographs, sculptures, ceramics, fiber art, woodwork, and jewelry in America. There are four distinct fairs, each with its own vibe, going on at once and a wide array of sidewalk sales and street performances to entertain you when you need a break. (And you will need to take breaks!) When hunger strikes, you're just steps away from many of Ann Arbor's best restaurants.

To plan your trip, order an art fair guide from the local visitors bureau at annarbor.org.

Ann Arbor Street Art Fair
artfair.org

Ann Arbor Summer Art Fair
theguild.org/fair/ann-arbor-art-fair

South University Art Fair
a2southu.com/art-fair

State Street Art Fair
statestreetdistrict.org/fair

TIP

The closest parking spots are in neighborhoods surrounding the fairs. Unfortunately, local parking rules prohibit long-term parking in these locations by nonresidents. To avoid getting a ticket (or a tow), drive to Briarwood Mall or Huron High School. You can park in either place for free; a small fee will get you a shuttle ride to the action.

DO THE DIAG
ON U-M'S CENTRAL CAMPUS

It's hard to imagine a more iconic location at the University of Michigan than The Diag (originally called the Diagonal Green), a large open space where the campus first began. Amid the crisscrossing sidewalks, you may see students relaxing between classes, signing up for campus clubs, or advocating for social change. (Organizers of an event called Hash Bash have promoted marijuana law reform here for more than 40 years.)

Around The Diag's edges are some of the university's oldest buildings, including the President's House (1840), Tappan Hall (1894), the Dana Building (1903), and West Hall (1904). The middle of the space is marked by a brass M; legend has it that if freshmen step on the M before taking their first exam, they'll fail. Don't be surprised if you see students giving it a wide berth!

Bounded by S. State St., N. University Ave.,
S. University Ave., and Church St.

MAKE YOUR MARK
ON ANN ARBOR'S BIGGEST BOULDER

The District of Columbia has an obelisk honoring our first president. And Ann Arbor has a rock, or rather The Rock, as it's known. Deposited in the county during the last ice age, The Rock was brought into the city in 1932 to serve as the centerpiece of a park commemorating George Washington's 200th birthday. (The triangle of land where the boulder sits is named Washington Park.) All was good for 20 years, until a visiting Michigan State University fan painted the letters MSU on The Rock. Since then, barely a day has gone by when the big boulder hasn't been embellished with some sort of sentiment, including Go Blue in a dozen languages. You can paint it, too, though most people settle for just taking a selfie.

Corner of Washtenaw Ave. and Hill St.

DISCOVER
THE FAIRY DOORS OF DOWNTOWN

Are fairies afoot in Ann Arbor? Evidence suggests they are . . . and some may even make their home here! More than 20 businesses and the downtown library feature "fairy doors," tiny entryways less than a foot high, each decorated in its own unique way. Some have elaborate cornices, others distinctive stoops—and thoughtful passersby leave little gifts on those stoops to welcome the wee people to the city.

The first fairy door appeared in the home of graphic designer Jonathan Wright, but now they can be found throughout the city. A fan favorite situated in the Sweetwaters café on Washington Street invites you to look inside and see a tiny cup of tea cooling on a table. Maps of many doors are pictured on Wright's website, Urban Fairies Operations, where he also sells posters and books.

urban-fairies.com

TIP

A 2019 list of Ann Arbor fairy doors, compiled by the *Michigan Daily*, included the following sites. NOTE: The doors may be inside or outside a given building.

Ann Arbor District Library (343 S. Fifth Ave.)

The Ark

Bank of Ann Arbor (125 S. Fifth Ave.)

Crazy Wisdom Bookstore & Tearoom

Edward Jones (123 N. Ashley St.)

Found

The Himalayan Bazaar

Jefferson Market

Lily Grace Cosmetics

Michigan Theater

Muse Atelier Vintage

Nicola's Books

Red Shoes

Shinola

Sweetwaters (123 W. Washington St.)

Tree Town Pediatric Dentistry

Bob and Betty Beyster Building

C. S. Mott Children's Hospital

Harlan Hatcher Graduate Library

Institute for Social Research

Washtenaw Dairy

DON YOUR DIRNDL
FOR A VISIT TO GERMAN PARK

On the last Saturdays of June, July, and August, you're invited to visit the private grounds of the German Park Recreation Club— and you don't have to speak German to get in! The gates open at 4 p.m., which is the best time to claim a table and camp out for an evening of sausage, sauerkraut, spaetzle, and *spaß* (fun). Want to be close to live music and dancing? The best seats for that are inside the pavilions. The surrounding tree-lined areas are a bit quieter and more family-friendly; many regulars gather there to play cards or board games.

And what would a German picnic be without beverages to enjoy? Rest assured, you can purchase a variety of German wines and beers—the latter in cups or buckets.

5549 Pontiac Tr.
(734) 769-0048
germanpark.org

TAP YOUR TOES
AT THE AFRICAN AMERICAN FESTIVAL

For most of the 20th century, the intersection of East Ann and North Fourth was the city's black-owned business district, lined with barber shops, shoeshine parlors, dry cleaners, restaurants, blues bars, and pool rooms. To honor that heritage of entrepreneurship, the Cultural and Community Events Coalition hosts an African American Downtown Festival on the site the first Saturday in June. Dozens of vendors line the roadways to sell jewelry, artwork, clothing, and books, and a kids' corner entertains little ones with make-and-take crafts and face painting. Underneath it all is the driving beat of live bands performing jazz, gospel, hip-hop, and soul music. Bring your dancing shoes and a big appetite; food vendors are also part of the event.

Corner of N. Fourth Ave. and E. Ann St.
(734) 858-9121
a2festival.org

STEP INSIDE
A HOUSE THAT IS ICE-AGE OLD

At first glance, the grayish structure on Ann Arbor's south side looks like a common home built in the 1840s. But look closely and you'll see that it's anything but common. In fact, it was made from the rocky residue of glaciers that retreated during the last ice age. These rounded, hand-size rocks give the house—an Ann Arbor landmark—its name: Cobblestone Farm.

Cobblestone construction of this type is rare in America; fewer than 900 examples exist, and six of them are in Washtenaw County. Cobblestone Farm is the only local example open to tourists. When you go, take note of the quality of workmanship on each side of the house. The front façade features the finest masonry, with specially sized stones set in a decorative herringbone pattern.

2781 Packard Rd.
(734) 794-6230
a2gov.org/departments/Parks-Recreation/parks-places/cobblestone-farm

TIP

Are you a lover of local history, interested in how the area you're passing through came to be? Then take time to visit the following downtown museums. Hours and days of operation are different for each. Check their websites for details.

The Museum on Main Street chronicles the history of the county's many communities through theme-based exhibits that rotate frequently throughout the year.

The Kempf House Museum, a nationally recognized gem of Greek Revival architecture, interprets the personal history of musicians Reuben and Pauline Kempf and the famous people who visited their home.

The Argus Museum showcases a collection of products, including the popular C3 rangefinder model, produced locally from 1936 to 1969 by the Argus Camera Company.

Museum on Main Street
500 N. Main St.
(734) 662-9092
washtenawhistory.org

Kempf House Museum
312 S. Division St.
(734) 994-4898
kempfhousemuseum.org

Argus Museum
525 W. William St.
(734) 769-0770
facebook.com/ArgusMuseum

LEARN ABOUT
GERALD FORD AT HIS LIBRARY

Ever wanted to visit a presidential library? There are only 14 in the US, and one is in Ann Arbor. Located on U-M's North Campus, this facility serves as the official repository for papers and records associated with our 38th president.

Gerald Ford began his political career as a congressman from Grand Rapids, Michigan, and that's where his museum is situated. But the years he spent in Ann Arbor, earning a bachelor's degree in economics and playing center for the Wolverines football team, prompted him to locate his library here. Like many such facilities, it caters to researchers, but anyone can tour the permanent displays honoring President Ford and his wife, Betty. Check the website for events such as lectures, book talks, and film screenings in the auditorium.

1000 Beal Ave.
(734) 205-0555
fordlibrarymuseum.gov/visit-library.aspx

TRACE THE STEPS
OF 19TH-CENTURY FREEDOM SEEKERS

Between 1810 and 1850, thousands of enslaved people fled oppression in the South for the promise of freedom in the North. Michigan's proximity to Canada made it a prime destination for this exodus, which occurred along a network of secret routes called the Underground Railroad. And three of those routes crisscrossed in the Ann Arbor area.

The African American Cultural and Historical Museum has preserved this important history in bus tours that take you past the homes of "station masters" who sheltered seekers, a schoolhouse that educated those who settled in this abolitionist stronghold, the building where a leading antislavery newspaper was published, and more. To provide context for all you see and hear, visit the museum itself, located in a north-side neighborhood steeped in early African American history.

1528 Pontiac Tr.
(734) 761-1717
aachm.org

FLY A FLAG
FOR LGBTQ PRIDE

The rainbow flags fly free during the Ann Arbor Pride celebration, an August fundraiser for the local LGBTQ community center. The weekend typically kicks off with a pre-party at a local nightclub on Friday. Saturday's activities take place along Catherine Street between Main Street and Fourth Avenue, with a beer garden, food trucks, and stage performances including DJs, dancers, poets, and local legends such as the Out Loud Chorus. A drag revue is typically scheduled for the evening. Sunday is reserved for the Pride Picnic, held at nearby Wheeler Park. With a goal of promoting acceptance within the larger community, picnic organizers provide food, drink, and family-friendly activities like face painting and a bounce house.

Catherine Street and other locations
annarborpride.com

DIG INTO
ANCIENT HISTORY AT THE KELSEY

From the outside, the Kelsey Museum of Archaeology looks like the oldest building on campus. (It's not.) But inside, it holds some of the oldest man-made artifacts on earth. The Kelsey is the showplace for the university's collection of objects excavated by faculty from ancient sites around the Mediterranean. Some of the objects you'll see on display at this free museum are ornamental. Others are functional. Then there are the ones associated with rituals, like burial. Did you know that early Egyptians mummified animals as well as humans? (Ask to see the cat in the Upjohn Exhibit Wing.) One of the museum's most popular artifacts is the elaborately painted mummy case of a high priest named Djehutymose. Djehutymose is much-loved outside Ann Arbor as well, as evidenced by his own Twitter account!

434 S. State St.
(734) 764-9304
lsa.umich.edu/kelsey

EXPLORE LIFE
AT A NATURAL HISTORY MUSEUM

In 2019, U-M opened a renewed museum of natural history in a striking space within the Biological Sciences Building. Gone are the static displays of minerals and animal mounts. In their place are colorful, engaging exhibits that translate big concepts like evolution and biodiversity into lessons even a young child can understand. Interactivity is around every corner, enabling you to step into the footprint of a mastodon (a skeletal pair of these guards the entry atrium), build a strand of DNA, and learn how to use lab tools. Want to talk to a real researcher? Attend one of their lectures or visit with them at the Science at Work labs located on the first and second floors.

Parking can be found at the structure behind the museum on Palmer Drive.

1105 N. University Ave.
(734) 764-0478
lsa.umich.edu/ummnh

TIP

When you're done learning
about life on Earth, take some
time to explore the solar system at
the university's two planetariums. One is
located inside the Museum of Natural History;
a fee is required for this activity.
The planetarium at Angell Hall is free.

Museum of Natural History Planetarium
1105 N. University Ave.
(734) 764-0478
lsa.umich.edu/ummnh/visitors/planetarium-dome-theater

Angell Hall Planetarium
435 S. State St.
(734) 764-3440
lsa.umich.edu/astro/public-outreach

SEE THE STARS
AT THE DETROIT OBSERVATORY

It's hard to imagine now, but the location of the Detroit Observatory in the midst of U-M's busy medical campus was once remote enough to provide a dark-sky setting for the practice of astronomy. Finished in 1854 using funds raised from wealthy Detroit benefactors (hence the name), the observatory is America's oldest still operating with its original equipment in place. And, as exhibits explain, 21 asteroids and two comets were discovered over the years at this venerable viewing spot. Want to see the sky for yourself? Open houses vary with the season; consult the website for dates.

NOTE: Parking is a challenge in the area; the nearest public structure is two blocks southeast on E. Medical Center Drive. But there is a drop-off point on the building's Observatory Drive side.

1398 E. Ann St.
(734) 764-3440
lsa.umich.edu/astro/public-outreach

TIP

Still starstruck? In addition to the Detroit Observatory, the university operates two others that offer public viewing hours:

Angell Hall Observatory
435 S. State St.
(734) 764-3440
lsa.umich.edu/astro/public-outreach

Peach Mountain Observatory
10280 N. Territorial Rd.
(734) 975-3248
umich.edu/~lowbrows

APPRECIATE
U-M'S IMPRESSIVE ART MUSEUM

In 1856, years before the art museums of Detroit, Toledo, and Chicago were founded, U-M established a free art gallery on campus to benefit its students and the community. Today that institution, known as the University of Michigan Museum of Art, possesses and preserves over 20,000 objects from Western, Asian, and African traditions as well as modern and contemporary art. But it's still free and still very public-oriented. In fact, UMMA recently invited the public to view an exhibit of 1,000 photographs and decide which of them should be purchased for the museum's permanent collection. Other engaging activities include poetry readings, music and dance performances in the soaring Tisch Apse, even story time for young patrons. In short, it's everything you'd expect from a big-city museum, right here in Ann Arbor.

525 S. State St.
(734) 764-0395
umma.umich.edu

EXAMINE
A UNIQUE DENTISTRY MUSEUM

Did you know that early dentists had to foot-pump a pedal to make their drills spin? That cocaine was once advertised as an anesthetic? Or that the University of Michigan pioneered the education of dental hygienists in the state beginning in 1921? These facts and more are revealed when you visit Ann Arbor's most unusual cultural attraction: the Sindecuse Museum of Dentistry. Tucked inside the W. K. Kellogg Institute Building on U-M's Central Campus, this museum named for a generous dental school alumnus celebrates the development of American dental techniques and technologies from the 18th century to today. Enjoy displays from the collection of more than 15,000 artifacts. And don't miss the 19th-century portrait of Apollonia, the patron saint of dentistry, whose story of tooth pain puts all others to shame!

1011 N. University Ave.
(734) 763-0767
sindecusemuseum.org

TIP
Though you might be tempted to park at the U-M structure just to the north of the Kellogg Building, don't do it. It's for dental school patients, faculty, and staff only. Metered street parking is your best bet.

STOP AND SHOP
AT THE WESTSIDE ART HOP

In Ann Arbor, you gotta have art. And if it isn't July, when the four big fairs combine into one wonderful weekend, what do you do? One answer is to go on the Westside Art Hop. For a single day in May and again in October, local artists on the west side of the city open their studios to the public, and visiting artists share spaces in neighbors' porches, garages, and yards. The artwork and crafts are juried, so the faces sometimes change. But you can be sure to find painters and potters as well as fiber artists, photographers, and jewelry designers—even a découpeur or two. Most of the artists exhibit between Eberwhite and Bach Elementary Schools, an easily walkable area with plenty of parking.

westsidearthop.com

TAKE A TOUR
OF MOTAWI TILEWORKS

It'll take only an hour of your time, but oh, the things you'll learn during the free Tuesday and Thursday tours of Motawi Tileworks! With a docent as your guide, you'll move from station to station throughout the studio, meeting the talented crafters who turn raw clay into radiant, hand-colored art and architectural pieces. Some, like the nature-themed tiles, are based on founder Nawal Motawi's original designs. Others are produced with permission from the estate of wildlife artist Charley Harper and the Frank Lloyd Wright Foundation. Samples of all may be purchased in the studio shop, with factory seconds available at a discount.

Want to try your hand at decorating a tile? Register for one of Motawi's monthly glazing workshops.

170 Enterprise Dr.
(734) 231-0017
motawi.com

WANDER
THE VERDANT WAVE FIELD

Remember Maya Lin, the Yale undergrad who won the design competition for the Vietnam Veterans Memorial in Washington, DC? That was the first step in her illustrious career as a sculptor of thought-provoking art in important locations across the country. In 1995, Lin brought her talents to Ann Arbor to honor the memory of a U-M aerospace engineering alumnus whose life was cut short. The result, called Wave Field, is an earthen sculpture found southeast of the François-Xavier Bagnoud Building on North Campus. This piece of art invites interaction. Pack a picnic to spread out among the grassy hollows, and let the kids run up and down its hills. That's what the sculptor intended. "It's a sanctuary," Lin explained, "yet it's playful."

Near the corner of Beal Ave. and Hayward St.
arts.umich.edu/museums-cultural-attractions/wave-field

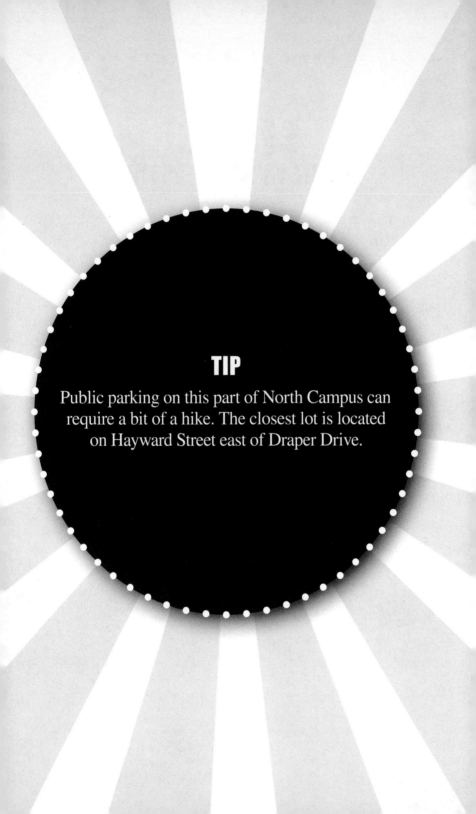

TIP

Public parking on this part of North Campus can require a bit of a hike. The closest lot is located on Hayward Street east of Draper Drive.

SAY YES!
TO THE YA'SSOO FESTIVAL

You may never get to Greece, but you can "visit" this Mediterranean country and its culture at an annual festival hosted by St. Nicholas Greek Orthodox Church. Held each June on the church grounds, Ya'ssoo (which means *good health*) is eagerly anticipated for its entrées—including pastitsio, souvlaki, and spanakopita—but it's the hand-made desserts that bring people back. Can't decide what to try? Buy a St. Nick's Mix sampler box to enjoy. Then settle down under the big-top tents to watch parish youth perform Greek folk dances to the accompaniment of a traditional bouzouki band.

Before you leave the festival, take time to tour the interior of the church and be awed by the hand-painted iconography adorning the walls and dome.

3109 Scio Church Rd.
(734) 332-8200
annarborgreekfestival.org

WALK AROUND
THE HALLOWED LAW QUAD

U-M is blessed with many beautiful buildings. If you're looking for a little bit of Oxford in Ann Arbor, the Law Quad is the place to go. Fashioned from granite and limestone in the English Gothic style, the William W. Cook Law Quadrangle takes up two city blocks and encompasses everything students need for living, learning, studying, and socializing. One must-see space is the original reading room of the Legal Research Building, with sky-high windows illuminating the literature. (A replacement library was built underground so as not to detract from the Quad's medieval appearance.) Then stroll around the courtyard, and see if you can find all 22 corbels honoring aspects of university life such as past presidents, academic pursuits, athletics, and the four seasons.

625 S. State St.
(734) 764-0537
law.umich.edu/aboutus/Pages/quad

SHOPPING AND FASHION

FIND YOUR FIT
AT MAST, A SHOE STORE THAT CARES

Many shoe stores have come and gone in Ann Arbor retail history. Still, Mast Shoes continues to prosper. What's the secret of their success? It boils down to one thing: personalized fit. As third-generation owner Molly Mast-Koss explains, "We are specially trained in this area." Not only do Mast staffers measure your feet, they also observe the way you walk, actually studying your biomechanics. This is especially critical if you have foot issues that can't be addressed at a chain store. Whatever brings you in the door, Molly says, the goal is "to help customers— all of our customers—find something that is both stylish and comfortable." With a range of brands including Naot, Ecco, Dansko, Merrell, and New Balance, and about 10,000 pairs of shoes in stock, this shouldn't be a problem!

2519 Jackson Ave. (Westgate Shopping Center)
(734) 662-8118
mastshoes.com

STROLL THROUGH
A2'S VINTAGE NICKELS ARCADE

In the early 20th century, Tom Nickels purchased land between State and Maynard Streets to build a structure housing a variety of stores under one roof. By 1918, his Nickels Arcade was complete, and people streamed in from miles around to experience this elegant, European-influenced prototype of a shopping mall. At its tile-clad State Street entrance stands the oldest business: Van Boven Inc. menswear (1921), dedicated to the quality craftsmanship and customer service of an earlier era. The Caravan Shop (1927), with its eclectic collection of gift items from around the world, anchors the west end. And in the skylit space in between, you'll find a tobacconist, an antiques store, a coffee house, a florist, a picture framer, and more.

Nickels Arcade
326–330 S. State St.

The Caravan Shop
(734) 668-6047
facebook.com/pages/category/Gift-Shop/Caravan-Gift-Shop

Van Boven Inc.
(734) 665-7228
vanboven.com

DICKER WITH DEALERS
AT THE A2 ANTIQUES MARKET

Need one more piece to complete your collection of jadeite, or a mid-century modern coffee table, or Justin Verlander's rookie baseball card? Since 1968, residents and visitors alike have shopped for items like these at the Ann Arbor Antiques Market. The market, located at the Washtenaw Farm Council Grounds, is a one-stop shopping event where dealers from around the country bring their wares to you. You can test out a sofa, feel the fabric of a vintage dress, or inspect the inner workings of a mechanical toy—all before you buy!

Bring the family and make a day of it; admission is $6 for adults and children get in free.

The antiques market is open on select weekends from April through October. Consult the website for this year's schedule.

5055 Ann Arbor-Saline Rd. (Washtenaw Farm Council Grounds)
(734) 678-0173
annarborantiquesmarket.com

TIP

Interested in old books? May is the month to attend the Ann Arbor Antiquarian Book Fair, a one-day event held in the ballroom of U-M's Michigan Union. Dozens of vendors from around the state and the country offer a wide range of material, including collectible Americana, literature, children's books, scholarly reference works, antiquarian maps, prints, and postcards. The $5 admission fee benefits the university's William L. Clements Library.

530 S. State St. (Michigan Union)
(734) 995-1891
annarborbookfair.com

STOCK UP
AT EAST-SIDE ETHNIC FOOD SHOPS

In the 1940s and '50s, the area near the intersection of Packard and Platt was the center of a small city named East Ann Arbor. Today many of its commercial buildings are occupied by ethnic grocers from the Middle and Far East. At 8,000 square feet, the Galleria Asian Market is the largest of these in terms of size and selection. But this isn't a big-box store. The staff is more than happy to come out from behind the counter to make menu suggestions and even throw samples of sweets into your bag as you exit. (Red bean mochi, anyone?) Deli items like banchan and kimbap are made fresh daily by the owner's wife, contributing to the mom-and-pop atmosphere.

3111 Packard St.
(734) 975-8900

In addition to the Galleria, six other such markets may be found in the neighborhood.

Aladdin's Market
3188 Packard St.
(734) 971-2150

Bombay Grocers
3010 Packard St.
(734) 971-7707

Golam Meat Market
3150 Packard St.
(734) 973-8486

Goodies Produce
3184 Packard St.
(734) 477-0772

Hyundai Asian Market
3893 Platt Rd.
(734) 929-6519

Mediterranean Market
4019 Stone School Rd.
(734) 477-8023

SHOP NEPAL
WITHOUT EVER LEAVING THE STATE

Ann Arbor rises only 840 feet above sea level. But when you visit the Himalayan Bazaar, you'll feel transported to the highest elevations of the fabled mountain range. At the front of the store, you'll find exotic gifts imported from Nepal, such as singing bowls and tingsha (finger cymbals), colorful Buddha busts, and hand-woven woolens. At the back of the store, your eyes will be drawn to a huge TV showing videos of climbing expeditions—a real you-are-there experience—as well as an Everest display of photos, flags, and gear used by the Bazaar's owners: Ann Arbor native Heather O'Neal and Pem Dorjee Sherpa. (If you like what you see, you can make arrangements at the store to accompany Heather on one of her twice-yearly treks to the southern Himalayas.)

218 S. Main St.
(734) 997-7229
thehimalayanbazaar.com

TIP

Heather and Pem are also connected through her short-term rental property (himalayanlodge.com) and his Himalayan-themed restaurant, Everest Sherpa.

GET COMFY
IN CLOTHING FROM COLLECTED WORKS

The comment most often heard from shoppers who enter the Collected Works boutique is, "These clothes must be comfortable." The soft, flowing fabrics, the thoughtful details and closures; these are not Gen Z's skin-skimming fashions. And they're not intended to be. The clothing lines that Collected Works carries, including Bryn Walker, Niche Clothing, Sympli, and Tianello, are designed for a more mature woman. But they also appeal to anyone who believes that clothing can be art. The pieces can easily be dressed up or down. And, if you like, a salesperson can suggest combinations for you to try. At the end of your shopping experience, you can walk out the door with an entire outfit— complete with a hat, a scarf, and jewelry.

303 Detroit St.
(734) 995-4222
collectedworksannarbor.com

EXPECT THE UNUSUAL
INSIDE ABRACADABRA

It's been said that *abracadabra* means "I will create as I speak." And that's exactly how Steven Lesse operates his jewelry design studio of the same name. He and his staff engage in collaborative conversations with their clients, believing that such communication is "central to intentional jewelry design that will stand the test of time." Looking for a unique gem for earrings? The Abra team might suggest white sapphires or moonstones—perhaps even something that Steven himself mined. Interested in exploring new materials for wedding bands? Abra has worked with everything from meteorite to maple wood. Alongside custom work, the studio features jewelry made by local artists, exclusive national designers, and fair-trade international artisans who share Steven's high ethical and environmental standards.

205 E. Liberty St.
(734) 994-4848
abragem.com

119

FIND THE FUN
AT ROCK PAPER SCISSORS

"We love paper and the perfect gift!" That quote, from the owner of Rock Paper Scissors, perfectly describes what you'll find inside this downtown gift shop. Brides-to-be stop in for save-the-date cards, engraved invitations, and custom-designed paper products. U-M fans look for what's new in the line of "Hail Yes!" products: hats, scarves, socks, and more. And then there are the greeting cards, naughty *and* nice, for every occasion. Rock Paper Scissors is also famous for its themed gift boxes. Know anyone who likes Moscow Mules? They'll love the box that contains cocktail syrup, an ice-cube mold, a copper shaker and mug set, *and* the staff's favorite mule recipe. With so much inventory in this store, you'll be hard-pressed not to find something to give or keep.

216 S. Main St.
(734) 531-6264
rockpaperscissorsshop.com

GEAR UP
AT BIVOUAC'S GREAT OUTDOORS STORE

There's a place in town where you can buy everything from crampons to cookstoves and all the clothing you'll need to look like an adventurer—and it's called Bivouac. Established in 1971, Bivouac has grown to fill four storefronts with outdoor merchandise for men, women, kids, and even dogs. The store's management believes in stocking high-quality products, which sometimes come with high prices. But they offset that with a price-match guarantee and a sale area on the lower level for even greater savings. If you have no time to shop but an idea of what you need, give the store a call. A Bivouac staffer will shop for you, then present all the items for your review—at no cost. Service like that is what separates this retailer from the chain stores.

336 S. State St.
(734) 761-6297
bivouacannarbor.com

SPEND A DAY
IN THE SHOPS OF KERRYTOWN

In the early 1980s, when contractor Joe O'Neal purchased a couple of old brick buildings on the near north side, people had a hard time imagining what he'd do with them. Flash forward to today, and you'll find he fashioned them into one of the city's most distinctive shopping centers: Kerrytown Market & Shops.

The first level of the main building has the feel of a European food market, with meat, fish, produce, and baked goods being sold from stalls. Floor two is filled with boutique spaces, including 16 Hands art gallery, Spun yarn shop, and Mudpuddles toy store (where the owners won't sell anything they haven't already play-tested!). Across a courtyard is Found, a unique collection of modern and vintage items that its proprietor "finds" at everything from arts and crafts fairs to estate sales.

Kerrytown Market & Shops, 407 N. Fifth Ave., kerrytown.com

16 Hands, (734) 761-1110, 16handsannarbor.com

Found, (734) 302-3060, foundgallery.com

Mudpuddles, (734) 662-0022, kerrytown.com/mudpuddles

Spun, (734) 780-7867, spunannarbor.com

TIP

Nestled in the midst of the Kerrytown buildings is the Ann Arbor Farmers Market, a local landmark that has connected growers with grateful customers since 1919. Fresh fruits and vegetables are sold there as well as artisanal cheeses, baked goods, nuts, maple syrup, and seasonal bouquets. Market day is every Saturday, with Wednesday added from May through December. On the first Wednesday evening of each month from May through October, the market hosts a food truck rally featuring live music.

315 Detroit St.
(734) 794-6255
a2farmersmarket.org

PLAY IT AGAIN
AT THE ENCORE RECORDS STORE

Whether you want to sell used vinyl (you know, the musical medium of the first three quarters of the 20th century?) or buy it, Encore Records is the place to go. Situated in a storefront just a block off Main Street, Encore is packed with vinyl – 33s, 45s, even 78s – in every conceivable musical genre. What floor space is left is given over to other media like CDs, DVDs, and Blu-ray discs as well as sheet music, books on music, and memorabilia. Don't see what you're looking for? The knowledgeable staff can help you find your way. (They also maintain a Discogs online store you can review before your visit.) If you've got the time, check out the new arrivals bin near the front door. And enjoy the browse, dude!

208 N. Fourth Ave.
(734) 662-6776
encorerecordsa2.com

FIND A FOSSIL
INSIDE FOUR DIRECTIONS

Looking for a piece of home décor that makes a statement in your space? Nothing says OMG quite like amethyst—an amethyst geode the size of a grown man! Or a fossilized fish embedded in sandstone. Or a slice of nautilus shell, polished to perfection. You can find these and other natural wonders at Main Street's Four Directions store. Owners Alan and Karen Freedman roam the world to collect these one-of-a-kind pieces and bring them to Ann Arbor for your approval. Interspersed among such objects in the store are striking examples of pottery, gemstone globes, and hand-hammered metal art. For personal adornment, the Freedmans offer a wide selection of jewelry, from pieces that incorporate Michigan Petoskey stones to Baltic amber in all its hues.

211 S. Main St.
(734) 996-9250
fourdirectionsa2.com

SHOP M DEN
FOR OFFICIAL U-M GEAR AND GIFTS

Ask any alum: A trip to the M Den is a must when you're in town. The Den is the official retailer of U-M's athletic department and the place to find nearly any maize-and-blue item you (or lucky gift recipients) desire. Michigan jerseys, T-shirts, sweatshirts, and hats are here. And so are some surprising offerings, like license plate covers and a meat seasoning rub! M Den also operates a more upscale establishment next to its State Street store. Called The Victors Collection, it includes clothing and merchandise co-branded with top-tier retailers like Dooney & Burke (handbags), Tommy Bahama (resort wear), and Shinola (watches). Whatever you buy, at whichever M Den store you choose, will help Michigan Athletics build more winning Wolverine teams.

mden.com

Briarwood Mall
656 Briarwood Cir., (734) 769-7455

Downtown
315 S. Main St., (734) 997-8000

State Street Area
303 S. State St., (734) 686-3002

The Victors Collection
307 S. State St., (734) 436-8138

HEAD DOWNTOWN
TO THE BAKING-AND-BULBS STORE

Downtown Home & Garden is hard to categorize but easy to love. As one customer described it, "I can get tulip bulbs, a bird house, a winter hat shaped like a Christmas tree, a cookie sheet, and a loaf of bread all in one place." Set aside time to comb through cookware and clothing—where pieces from Carhartt, Filson, and Stormy Kromer fill the shelves—as well as handcrafted toys. In spring and summer, customers drive right into the building to pick up topsoil and trays of seedlings. In the fall, holiday decorations take over. No matter the season, there's something to enjoy, especially around the checkout counter where coffee and pastries can be purchased. That's also where you'll spot the store's "security officer," a red tabby named Wallace.

210 S. Ashley St.
(734) 662-8122
downtownhomeandgarden.com

TIP
On select evenings from March through October, Downtown Home & Garden transforms its fenced-in parking lot into Bill's Beer Garden. You can enjoy beer, wine, mixed drinks, and soft drinks at this family-friendly venue, sometimes called The Community's Backyard.

READ AWAY
AT THE AWARD-WINNING LITERATI

It was the closing of Ann Arbor-based Borders bookstore that convinced Michael and Hilary Gustafson to leave their life in Brooklyn and move back to Michigan to fill the gap. Local bibliophiles are glad they did. The couple has brought an indie vibe to the business of book selling. Their Literati Bookstore has grown by leaps and bounds as a result, now boasting a collection of 30,000 books spread out over three floors. But it wasn't sheer volume (pun intended) that prompted *Publishers Weekly* to name Literati its bookstore of the year for 2019. It was the care the Gustafsons put into curating the contents of Literati and the way the store's events—author visits, book clubs, and "local learning" classes—build a sense of community among its customers.

124 E. Washington St.
(734) 585-5567
literatibookstore.com

TIP
Since Literati's inception, an old typewriter has sat on a table as an experiment to see what people might type if they felt free to leave a message. Thousands of people have responded to this invitation, with comments ranging from goofy ("Where's the power button?") to gut-wrenching ("I'm the best book ever written. And most of the people I've loved just can't read."). In 2018, Michael Gustafson and designer Oliver Uberti published a collection of their favorites in a book titled *Notes from a Public Typewriter*.

Ann Arbor is blessed with a bounty of bookstores. In addition to Literati, current booksellers include:

Barnes & Noble
3235 Washtenaw Ave.
(734) 973-0846
barnesandnoble.com

Bookbound
1729 Plymouth Rd.
(734) 369-4345
bookboundbookstore.com

Crazy Wisdom Bookstore & Tearoom
114 S. Main St.
(734) 665-2757
crazywisdom.net

Nicola's Books
2513 Jackson Ave.
(734) 662-0600
nicolasbooks.com

Our Lady of Grace Bookstore
24 Frank Lloyd Wright Dr., Lobby C
(734) 930-3747
ourladyofgracebookstore.com

CELEBRATE
COMIC BOOK CULTURE AT THE VAULT

Did you know that the world's best comic shop is located in Ann Arbor? Vault of Midnight received that honor at a recent ComicCon, and when you step inside the space, you'll understand why. Vault's thoughtfully curated collection—which is complemented by graphic novels, board games, models, action figures, toys, and apparel—is top-shelf. And so are its people: self-described "ambassadors for all things geeky" who present their wares as "the awesome, fun, and universally accessible pieces of entertainment that they are." Fanboys are frequent customers, but Vault strives to appeal to fangirls, too . . . *and* it's dedicated an entire section of the store to titles that children will love (and parents will approve of). Check out the shop's Super Skull comic book podcast highlighting new releases, reviews, and industry intel.

219 S. Main St.
(734) 998-1413
vaultofmidnight.com

SEEK SERENITY
AND CHÈVRE AT WHITE LOTUS FARMS

It might be the scenic koi pond. Or the unique statuary. Or the colorful flower beds that line the driveway. By the time you park your car, you'll realize this is not your typical farmstead. White Lotus Farms has a meditative quality to it, which is not surprising given that it's operated by a community of Buddhists. Their values influence their agricultural practices, and it shows in the quality of the products they make. For instance, a herd of happy goats are the source of WLF's award-winning chèvre. Organic grains go into their mouthwatering Oh! pastry, a cross between a donut and a croissant. And their hand-tended microgreens are many times more nutritious than their mature counterparts. Take a tour of the operation to hear how these folks integrate faith and farming.

7217 W. Liberty Rd.
(734) 707-1284
whitelotusfarms.com

TIP
White Lotus Farms is open to the public on Saturdays all year round, but their food and a line of botanical body products are also available for purchase at the Ann Arbor Farmers Market.

ENJOY THE AMBIENCE
AT WEST SIDE BOOK SHOP

Outside, West Side Book Shop looks like it was plucked from London's Charing Cross Road and plopped down onto Ann Arbor's Liberty Street without a scratch. Inside, it's everything a rare/used bookstore should be: titles in bookcases rising to the ceiling (and some in stacks on the floor) covering subjects both popular and obscure, with an expert owner on hand to guide you on your journey of discovery. Jay Platt is that owner, and he has been since 1975. His favorite books deal with polar exploration, but he also offers a sizable collection of titles in general travel, Americana, modern first editions, mysteries, and detective fiction. The store's back room is an unexpected delight, with drawers of old maps and original photographs, including works by Edward S. Curtis, who focused his lens on Native Americans.

113 W. Liberty St.
(734) 995-1891
facebook.com/pages/West-Side-Book-Shop

Ann Arborites recognize the value of preserving the written word and have patronized a variety of rare/used bookstores over the years. Current merchants include:

Dawn Treader
514 E. Liberty St.
(734) 995-1008
dawntreaderbooks.com

Friends Bookshop
(inside the downtown Ann Arbor District Library)
343 S. Fifth Ave.
(734) 302-7774
faadl.org

Motte & Bailey Booksellers
212 N. Fourth Ave.
(734) 669-0451
mottebooks.com

SUPPORT AREA NONPROFITS
AT THE KIWANIS SALE

It began in 1927 as a one-time-only fundraiser for local charities. More than 90 years later, the Kiwanis Sale is still going strong and recently had to upsize to a 90,000-square-foot warehouse to handle all the foot traffic. Run by the local chapter of this international service club, the sale features all types of furniture, sports and exercise equipment, toys, kitchen and household items, decorative objects, electronics, books and music, jewelry and clothing, collectibles, and seasonal decorations.

The building is open every Friday and Saturday from 9 a.m. to 1 p.m.; go early to beat the crowds and browse the contents. The Kiwanis Sale raises about $250,000 each year for area nonprofits benefiting children and families, providing basic needs support, education, transportation, counseling, camps, after-school tutoring, and therapy programs.

100 N. Staebler Rd.
(734) 665-0450
kiwanissale.com

In addition to the Kiwanis Sale, you'll find
great deals at these thrift stores as well:

Ann Arbor PTO Thrift Shop
2280 S. Industrial Ave.
(734) 996-9155

Ann Arbor Thrift Shop
3500 Washtenaw Ave.
(734) 662-6771

Goodwill Ann Arbor/Ypsilanti Store
3782 Carpenter Rd.
(734) 272-0667

Salvation Army Family Store
1621 S. State St.
(734) 332-3948

The ShareHouse
5161 Jackson Rd.
(734) 222-0876

St. Vincent de Paul Thrift Store
1001 Broadway St.
(734) 761-1400

SUGGESTED
ITINERARIES

AROUND-THE-WORLD EATS

Sample Central Europe at Amadeus, 2

Experience Ethiopia at The Blue Nile, 4

Enjoy French Food at the Surprising Spencer, 6

Savor the Flavors of Cuban-Style Frita Batidos, 10

Go Pan-Asian at the Pacific Rim, 13

Sink Your Teeth into a Mani Osteria Pizza, 14

Sip a Sangria at a True Spanish Restaurant, 18

Reach New Heights with the Food at Everest Sherpa, 32

ART AND ARCHITECTURE LOVER

Join A2 Modern on a Mid-Century Home Tour, 80

Visit Four Art Fairs in One Weekend, 82

Do The Diag on U-M's Central Campus, 84

Step Inside a House That is Ice-Age Old, 90

Appreciate U-M's Impressive Art Museum, 100

Stop and Shop the Westside Art Hop, 102

Take a Tour of Motawi Tileworks, 103

BOUNTY OF BEVERAGES

COOL FOR KIDS

MUSIC MAVEN

TAKE A TOUR

ACTIVITIES
BY SEASON

SPRING (MARCH-MAY)

SUMMER (JUNE-AUGUST)

FALL (SEPTEMBER-NOVEMBER)

WINTER (DECEMBER-FEBRUARY)

INDEX